Online Dating For Dummies

A Personal Journal of

What and Who to Avoid and Why

(Questions and Some Answers)

by

Jocelyn A. Brown, PhD

BSP Company

Boulder, Colorado

Online Dating for Dummies

Published in the United States by Brown and Sons Publishing, Boulder, Colorado

ISBN - 9781708118457 (paperback)

Nonfiction—Family & Relationships—Dating—Love and Romance

Cover image by Elsa Riva from Pixabay
Image, pg. 27, Gordon Johnson
Image, pg. 9 by Elsa Riva, Pixabay
Dedication line adapted from "God Only Knows" by For King and Country
All illustrations by emr cartoons except: pg. 3 by Vezhelka, pg. pg. 11 by Okta Chan, pg. 13 by Vinh Phan, pg. 77 by Tahir Khan

http://brownandsonspublishing.com

Dedication

For the lonely, for the afraid, the misunderstood, and the ones to blame.

Online Dating for Dummies

To find the right person, I must BE the right person.

Content

Online dating can be like getting on an endless carousel ride at the amusement park. It just goes around and around as you spot the same faces on each rotation. After awhile you just want to get off the damn thing and look for a better ride.

Introduction

Have you been scouring the different online dating sites for years, searching for new faces, new reasons to keep returning to the same pages and profiles? Have you come across the same old messages, the same demographics, the same old pictures, and the same old stories? Do you end up cancelling memberships in frustration, only to renew your subscriptions months later in hopes of finding, meeting someone new? Some have found love at these sites. Some have found dates. Some have found friends. So, you believe there is hope – if you just keep signing up and searching again . . . and again. It all becomes one desperate plea for a decent connection with a normal person. Following your frustrated hiatus, you forget about the dead end profiles that caused the frustration in the first place, so when you finally return, hopeful, you end up tapping into those same names and faces or those same types again. And they're returning to your same name and face. This may not be your specific scenario, but if you've been engaged with online dating sites for multiple years without desirable results, you may be wondering why. There may be multiple answers. This is a journey of self-discovery. Only you can answer the grand question, WHY?

Happy Discoveries!

Jocelyn A. Brown, PhD

WISH LIST MAKERS

These online dating members have profiles with lists of requirements for their potential dates. Often the lists are long and quite specific. And more often than not, the requirements are one-sided, based solely upon their needs from a partner with few or no requirements of themselves. Wish List Makers seem to look for perfection, conjuring up fantasy partners. These are unrealistic expectations. No member would be able to fulfill this subscriber's dreams. Better to leave this person to his/her imaginings.

CAPITAL COMMUNICATORS

Why do some online profiles roar at you in all capital letters? Sometimes it is just an oversight, but what is being conveyed is a shouting/yelling stance. The reader may feel that the person is aggressive or that the person needs to be heard LOUDLY. This need is particularly emphasized when the person uses capital letters throughout, but selectively de-capitalizes key words, indicating an intentional use. This could be a clear warning that the online dater is an aggressive, possibly angry person or that the person's need to be heard is overpowering. In either case, one should proceed with caution or move on to a less intense profile.

HAND SLAPPER SUBSCRIBERS

Hand Slappers remind online daters of all the things you are not allowed to do or shouldn't do if you want a response from them. You'd better not attempt to contact them if you don't have a photo or any number of issues they consider bothersome. It's especially off-putting when the profile begins with all the negatives. Even if you agree with the list of no-not, who would want to approach a potential date that leads off with a list of don'ts? Look for positive people instead.

WRETCHED RETURNERS

Ahh, they're back . . . Sometimes we leave a membership behind for a period of time to try out new sites, get a fresh perspective, or to get away from the same faces that keep cycling through. Hopefully, if we return, we are in a positive state of mind to begin anew. It can be depressing to read a profile that begins with pessimistic expectations. "Here I go again. I don't expect that my search will yield anything, but I'll give it one more try. . ." Yikes, and never mind. You get what you expect to get. This profile is a huge downer. Next!

SERIAL SUBSCRIBERS

This member has been on this site and probably multiple sites F O R E V E R. Nothing has changed – not the photos, not the profile – nada. There is no intention of actually meeting and forming relationships. This member makes a hobby of surfing the dating sites. Maybe the member is a lonely shut-in with good internet service. Maybe the person doesn't consider him/herself date-worthy or presentable enough to establish a real romantic connection. Whatever the case, it's a dead end for someone who is looking for a meet-up and possible love connection. Search for fresh prospects.

MONOLOGUE MANIACS

They just never stop writing. The profile goes on and on and on ad nauseam. By the time you finish reading, you've heard about their every ski trip, every one of their kids' graduations and career goals, and every hobby they've ever engaged in since grade school. You can be certain that any live, in-person conversation will be a soliloquy, rather than a dialogue. Sometimes less is more. Search for balance.

MUTE MEMBERS

Worse than the Monologue Maniacs, are the Mute Members, whose only profile message is, "Message me to find out more." Well, the whole point in reading through profiles is to find out more about a person. Then, one can decide if she/he wants to go further and send a message. The Mute Members' lack of communication is a strong indication that an engaging in-person connection is not likely to happen. If they can't demonstrate an ability to communicate on a dating site, they should find another medium, such as a phone chat line and you should find another profile to read.

FACELESS FUMBLEDUDS

Body pics are great! Especially Ab shots. But, please . . . a hot body alone can't trick us into forgetting there are no full-face images. What is being kept from us and why? Is it pure vanity that leads the member to think we would be so mesmerized by the photo of the body that we would run, panting, to establish communication? Or is the face image so unacceptable that it had to be excluded? Either way, omission is a huge red flag. Don't settle for that. Ask for a true glimpse into the soul through the eyes and face or bypass the butt shot profile.

EVERYTHING BUT

This online dating subscriber takes us on a scenic picture tour of her/his life. You get to see the Grand Canyon, the delicious and colorful dish that was eaten at the 5 star restaurant, and the manatees in the harbor where he/she vacationed. The only thing missing from the photo cache is the person. These days, there is no excuse for not including yourself in at least one photo opportunity. Mastering the selfie photo may take a little practice, but even a bad shot is better than no shot. So if a dating member is unable or unwilling to disclose his/her own image, everything is left up to the imagination. Imagine moving on to a profile with self-images.

13

PLEASE, PLEASE PROFILES

Begging sometimes works. Most times, it's just concerning. "Please pick me." "I'm a good catch. Really. If you select me, you won't be disappointed!" "I'm tired of being alone and I need someone so bad." Warning signs – neediness is not a good relationship building tool. If the connection leads to a date, there can be issues with clingy behaviors, co- dependency, and plain old, annoying insecurity. Needing or wanting love is not a problem. Pleading and begging can be a problem. While it may be flattering to the receiver initially, these behaviors can thwart long-term, positive relationships. Think twice before answering that call.

Write down one of these types that you have encountered.

Describe this type below.

What similarities do you share with this type?

Write down another of these types have you encountered.

Describe this type below.

What similarities do you share with this type?

Write down another one of these types have you encountered.

Describe this type below.

What similarities do you share with this type?

AFTERWORD

Ultimately, each online dater must decide which profiles and styles are to be pursued or avoided and how his or her own online persona should be revised. These peer insights are merely suggestions garnered from experience. You are the master or mistress of your own search for love. There are no guarantees, only opportunities. May your pursuits lead to happiness!

QUESTIONNAIRE

How many total years have you been using online dating sites?

What are your greatest fears with online

dating?

What do you hope for most in an encounter?

Describe your worst experience(s) on a

dating site?

What do you think are women's greatest
concerns about online dating?

What do you think are men's greatest
concerns about online dating?

Of the types listed in this book, which has
been the greatest challenge for you and
why?

Which types of sites do you find to be
the most reputable (i.e. fitness,
religious, culture-specific, etc.)?
Why?

Which types of sites do you find to be
the least reputable? Why?

What have you discovered about yourself in
the process of dating online?

What types of usernames catch your attention? Why? What types of usernames are unappealing? Why? What impressions do they leave?

Describe in detail the profile that you thought was your ideal.

What aspects of this person's profile suited you best?

What does your username reveal about you?

How long do you chat online with a person before exchanging personal contact information?

What do you need to know about a person before you are comfortable exchanging personal contact information?

How many members have you met in person?

Describe an in-person date that developed into a relationship.

Describe an in-person date that never developed beyond that point.

How many of the telephone conversations led to in-person meetings?

How many people have you met in person online?

When you find your ideal relationship, what do you hope to learn from the other person?

What would you like the other person to learn from you?

NOTES TO SELF - MY JOURNEY

Keeping a journal of your experiences, preferences, and expectations can help you pursue online dating with intentionality. Go on a 45 day personal quest to discover patterns and predicaments that define your online dating experience. Spend a minimum of 30 minutes a day connecting with different members from online dating sites. Do this for 45 days and write down your experiences each day in this journal. At the end of the 45 days, read through your notes and highlight any patterns you see from day to day. Who are you drawn to? Who responds to you? What traits interest you most? What is your mood before starting the search? After?

<u>MY JOURNEY</u> - <u>Day 1</u>

MY JOURNEY - Day 2

<u>MY JOURNEY - Day 3</u>

MY JOURNEY- Day 4

MY JOURNEY- Day 5

MY JOURNEY - Day 6

Online Dating for Dummies

<u>MY JOURNEY Day 7</u>

MY JOURNEY - Day 8

<u>MY JOURNEY</u> - Day 9

MY JOURNEY - Day 10

<u>MY JOURNEY - Day 11</u>

MY JOURNEY - Day 12

<u>MY JOURNEY - Day 13</u>

MY JOURNEY - Day 14

<u>MY JOURNEY - Day 15</u>

MY JOURNEY - Day 16

MY JOURNEY- Day 17

MY JOURNEY - Day 18

MY JOURNEY - Day 19

MY JOURNEY - Day 20

MY JOURNEY- Day 21

MY JOURNEY- Day 22

<u>MY JOURNEY</u> - <u>Day 23</u>

MY JOURNEY - Day 24

MY JOURNEY - Day 25

MY JOURNEY - Day 26

<u>MY JOURNEY - Day 27</u>

MY JOURNEY - Day 28

MY JOURNEY - Day 29

MY JOURNEY - Day 30

MY JOURNEY - Day 31

MY JOURNEY - Day 32

MY JOURNEY - Day 33

MY JOURNEY- Day 34

MY JOURNEY - Day 35

MY JOURNEY - Day 36

<u>MY JOURNEY - Day 37</u>

MY JOURNEY - Day 38

MY JOURNEY - Day 39

MY JOURNEY - Day 40

MY JOURNEY - Day 41

MY JOURNEY - Day 42

MY JOURNEY - Day 43

MY JOURNEY - Day 44

MY JOURNEY - Day 45

Your Profile:The Mirror

Take a moment to read through your profile on the dating sites you use.

How many relationship requirements in a partner do you list in your profile?

List your relationship requirements in a partner.

Which of those relationship requirements do you have?

How many dos/don'ts/shoulds/ shouldn'ts are listed in your profile?

List the dos/don'ts/shoulds/
shouldn'ts that are listed in your
profile.

What, if any, language is self-
defeating, depressing, or negative in
your profile.

What five adjectives come to mind
when you read your profile?

What examples and details about
yourself and your lifestyle do you
include in your profile?

What details about your lifestyle do you leave out of your profile?

What details about your personality do you leave out of your profile?

How old is your oldest photo on your profile?

On a scale of 1 - 5, with 5 being "great," what do you think your chances of finding a relationship through internet dating?

The person I want to find is the person I strive to be.

Made in the USA
Columbia, SC
06 December 2022

72893119R00046